Style NOT Fashion

By

Viviana Rullo

Fashions fade, style is eternal

— Yves Saint-Laurent

Introduction

Thanks for buying this book.

I hope it will guide you through the minefield that is the pursuit of developing your own personal style.

Unfortunately, we are all judged by the way we look, regardless if you are on the school run or in a boardroom. In all aspects of life, good presentation is a definite plus.

When you look well put-together, you immediately gain respect from others because you look as though you respect yourself.

When you have strong personal style you will feel more confident, which will help you in every area of your life. There is no stopping a confident woman.

In this book, I will endeavour to help you to say goodbye to having a closet full of clothes and nothing to wear. This book will guide you through building a working capsule wardrobe, knowing what suits you and how to get the designer gear you desire at a reasonable price via eBay.

Fashion and style should be fun, not a chore, even if you hate shopping.

Dedication

To my Dad, a true ball buster, who always did it his way and pushed me to do the same.

PS this is circa 1986 and before I took an interest in style. Yes, this was a cool look in NYC then.

1. Be a Stylish Frugalista

No, this is not an oxymoron. Just because you are watching your pennies doesn't mean there's an excuse for losing any sense of style that you possess. Being frugal is even more of a reason to dress well, because you cannot afford to make fashion mistakes. Clothing, it seems, is ruled by the 80/20 rule, which is: we wear 20 per-cent of our clothing 80 per-cent of the time.

I know that I have one dress that, whenever I put it on, makes me feel like I am one stylish gal. I think we all have that one item that makes us stand up a bit taller, hold our stomachs in and just feel like we can do anything. What we all need is an entire wardrobe of clothing like *that* dress.

I am a firm believer in 'less is more' in the wardrobe department. I personally don't like owning lots of clothes for the following reasons: it takes longer to decide what to wear in the morning;, your closet is more cluttered, which makes it harder to keep track of your clothes;, the process of changing over from one season to the next is more of a hassle and, after a career of shopping, I don't really enjoy it as much anymore.

I buy good pieces that will last me many seasons. I do not even go into cheap shops like Primark as I think they are a false economy. I have bought items there in the past that I have loved, then after two washes, they bobbled or fell apart. I know this might not be the most popular opinion, I have friends who adore the cheap-and-cheerful, but it is not for me.

I think there is a *huge* difference between style and fashion. Audrey Hepburn had style whereas Christina Aguilera works at being fashionable. Being in fashion is a sport for the rich. Who can afford to buy a new wardrobe every season? Who has the time, money or inclination? I prefer to be stylish (at least I hope so) which means you wearing the clothes, not the other way around.

Fashion is what you're offered four times a year by designers. And style is what you choose. — *Lauren Hutton*

2. Style vs Fashion

We all know what fashion is: it is the clothing and accessories that the media tells us will make us look good. It is what the celebrities are sporting, so of course we want a bit of that too. It is the hot-pink skinny jeans that won't look good on anyone over a size 8UK or a 4US or the handbag that costs three months' rent or mortgage.

I truly dislike that kind of fashion tyranny. It reeks of being bullied at school and never feeling quite good enough. I much prefer having style over being in fashion. Having the latest 'it bag' is one thing: having great personal style is quite another.

Many people think that being fashionable means having a bulging wardrobe. True style is feeling comfortable with your appearance. *You* should be the one that shines, not just the fashionable garb you have on your back.

There is a big difference between being a stylish individual and being in fashion.

Style vs Fashion

Style is timeless.	Fashion expires when the trend is over.
Style is exclusive to **you**.	Fashion is what the crowds are wearing.
Personal style evolves; you add to your collection.	Fashion needs to constantly be replenished: there is always a new trend to buy into.
When you stay true to your personal style, you always feel like yourself.	When you wear something a bit trendy, it is possible to feel like you are in costume or look like someone else.
True style is never out of style.	**In fashion, one day you are in and the next you are out.** – *Heidi Klum, Project Runway*

Style is knowing who you are, what you want to say, and not giving a damn. — *Gore Vidal*

There are many people in fashion who hold on tightly to their personal style while telling us to buy the next big thing. Anna Wintour, for example, the editor of US *Vogue*, who you will never see in trousers or with a different hairstyle. Ms Wintour's hair is the epitome of her personal style.

Fashion is something you buy,
STYLE is something you OWN! — *Carine Roitfield*

The same applies for Carine Roitfield, the brilliant ex-editrix of Paris *Vogue*, who is known for her towering heels and smoky eye makeup. Again, another editor who you will rarely see in trousers: is this something we should note?

These women have been selling us high fashion for more than a decade and they both march to the beat of their own style drum. Is it time for us ladies to decide what our personal style is? We should know which styles and shapes suit us and, possibly more importantly, what doesn't.

Fashions fade, style is eternal. — *Yves Saint-Laurent*

No one is born stylish; it is something that develops with your personality and time. In the next part we will go over how to find your personal style, and if you are still thinking that you would rather be fashionable, here is another quote from a true original.

Fashion is what you adopt when you don't know who you are. — *Quentin Crisp*

Fashion can be bought. Style one must possess. — *Edna Woolman Chase, Vogue Editor 1914-1952*

3. Finding your Personal Style

I know so many women with bulging closets and still nothing to wear. I have already mentioned the 20/80 rule: wearing 20 per-cent of your clothes 80 per-cent of the time. I think we ladies are too spoiled for choice, with all the inexpensive high street retailers around, and we are getting into debt because of it. It is so easy to wander into Primark or H&M and buy a silver sparkly dress when you are usually in sombre black and it is so easy to justify, since it was only £25/$45.

What happened to personal style? I want a wardrobe that complements me, not overpowers me. I want statement pieces. I want to look like me, not five different people in a week.

You gotta have style. It helps you get up in the morning. It's a way of life. Without it you're nobody. - *Diana Vreeland*

Tips on finding your personal style

What is your best dress or outfit?

Go through your wardrobe and pull out **the** garment that makes you feel amazing when you wear it. What is so special about it? The cut? The colour? The neckline? Do you feel like Carrie Bradshaw? Audrey Hepburn? Kate Moss? Or another icon? Build on this knowledge to plan your personal style.

- **Find your own style and have the courage to stick to it.**
- **Choose your clothes for your way of life.**
- **Make your wardrobe as versatile as an actress. It should be able to play many roles.**
- **Find your happiest colours – the ones that make you feel good.**
- **Care for your clothes, like the good friends they are! —** *Joan Crawford*

The best color in the whole world, is the one that looks good, on you! — *Coco Chanel*

Know your palette

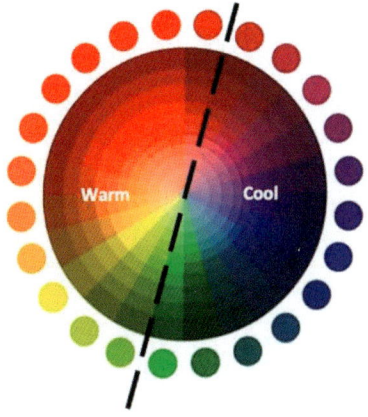

I have found so many of my fashion mistakes are made by purchasing an item in an unflattering colour. There are a few colour rules:

- Figure out if you are a warm-coloured or a cold-coloured person. This is easy to figure out. Usually if you like the look of gold next to your skin, you are a warm-toned person and the opposite if you prefer silver. This also works with white versus cream: white is a cold colour and cream a warm one, one looks fabulous and the other will washes the colour from your face.

- Never wear the colour that you are. The fabulous wardrobe czar, Annabel Hodin, said that to me and it totally holds true. If you have pale skin and blond hair, yellow will most likely not be a good choice: you might look like a banana.

- As we get a bit older, we cannot fall back on the "black goes with everything" theory. Most people should wear a bit of colour next to their face, especially in the winter when we all look a bit pale. If you look at television presenters, most of them wear a scarf or a flattering colour next to their faces. Anna Wintour is often seen sporting a colourful necklace to brighten up hers.

I've been 40 years discovering that the queen of all colors was black. — *Pierre-Auguste Renoir*

- Think about the items of clothing that get you the most compliments - if you always get a smile when you wear green, then maybe you should work on getting a few more green items in your wardrobe.

- Shop near the window: a lovely looking dress can look very different in the artificial light in the back of a shop, so take the garment to the front of the shop to see its true colour.

Get a role model

If you are not sure what would suit you, try finding someone who sort of looks like you. You will probably need two different role models: one for your colouring and one for your body shape.

Since I have covered colouring, let's talk about body type. There has been a bit of controversy about how many female body types there are: Trinny and Susannah have written The Body Shape Bible in which they describe twelve body shapes. Yes, twelve. Not the basic apple, pear, hourglass and boyish. I do think they have something there so if you are at all confused as to which shape you are, get yourself to the library immediately to have a look at their book. Knowing which shapes are best for your shape will save you time, money and possibly tears.

The great thing about having a role model, is the chance that they have paid the big bucks to a stylist to flatter their shape – so you can steal that information and hit the shops. Try to find a role model in your age range. There is no point loving what a 20-year-old is wearing if you are 42.

Know first, who you are; and then adorn yourself accordingly. — **Epictetus**

You need to take all the previous steps into consideration when you are discovering your personal style.

Here is a little recap:s

1. What is your all-time favourite garment?

2. Figure out your palette.

3. Get a role model.

4. Decluttering

Before you can start building your own personal style you must have a clear-out. I like to do a regular cull seasonally. You cannot objectively look at what you have when there are items that need to be thrown out or donated. You will not be able to see the wood through the trees.

Decluttering will make your life and getting dressed in the morning much easier. There is nothing worse than looking at a closet full of clothes with nothing to wear. I do not advocate the idea that if you have not worn a garment in six months you should chuck it. If you invest in expensive clothing, the chances are you will wear it for much longer than the average high street purchase. I have been known to find an item in the back of my wardrobe that is over 20 years old and it actually looks new again, but this generally only works with designer pieces that were not super on trend when you bought them.

How to declutter

When you sort out your closet, make three piles: to keep, to get rid of and to think about.

It is pretty easy to figure out what you want to keep – your favourite jeans, great sweaters, dresses that make you happy when you wear them, etc. What to get rid of include items that no longer suit your lifestyle, for example, miniskirts, crop tops, jeans that you will **never** fit into again and anything that is stained or damaged beyond repair. The most difficult, and probably the largest, pile will be the 'think about' one. In that pile you will have: the dress that you met your husband in but will never wear again; the designer piece that you spent too much on, but have never worn (yes, everyone has those, no matter how good a shopper you are); the sweater that is just not the right colour for you, etc.

You must be strict and honest with yourself about the 'think about' pile. It is all right to save a few sentimental pieces but any expensive items that you have not worn should go directly to a consignment shop or on eBay, so you can make a bit of your money back to invest in new clothes.

You will know in your heart if you are really ever going to wear something again: if the answer is 'no', then dump it.

Decluttering accessories - I never get rid of accessories- scarves, jewellery, sunglasses, handbags – because you never know when the right occasion to wear them might turn up.

Seasonal Decluttering

Winter decluttering – At the end of the winter, go through all your tights and socks to get rid of all the ones with holes and, in the case of tights, pulls. Some tights such as Spanx can be quite pricey so before I get rid of them I make sure I cannot get any more wear from them. If they have a hole in the foot, I will try to mend them or if they are only suitable to wear with boots, I put them in a plastic freezer bag labelled 'For Boots Only'.

When I buy socks, I buy all the same (brand and colour) so I can match them quickly and can make new pairs if some develop holes or get lost. This saves a lot of time and energy when getting dressed.

Summer decluttering – As it starts to get chilly, go through all your T-shirts: make the ones with any stains into rags and make a list of what you will need to replace in terms of layering options for the colder months. Get rid of old flip-flops and any sandals that are not in good enough condition to use the following year, and do the same for bathing suits, sun dresses– basically anything that looks shabby.

People with very big wardrobes might need to use the 'one in, one out' system – this is for people who find it hard to declutter or just like to shop too much. When you take this on, you cannot bring a new item in without getting rid of something old. I do this with my beloved, who collects Hawaiian shirts: he is not allowed to get a new one unless he gets rid of one that is falling apart.

You will feel much lighter after you have done your first big declutter. Your closet will be neater with only the clothes you actually wear and you will be able to see any gaps in your wardrobe.

5. Love a Uniform or the Myth of the Capsule Wardrobe

By this point, you have figured out which colours suit you, and you have picked out the garment that makes you feel like a million bucks. Now you want build your *Stylish Frugalista* wardrobe. We have all heard magazines talk about getting the ultimate capsule wardrobe, but where do you begin? What should you have in your capsule wardrobe?

The first thing, I can't stress enough, is don't buy into trends. When you are building a capsule wardrobe that you want to last a few seasons buy classic pieces and spend the most you can afford.

Reinvent new combinations of what you already own. Improvise. Become more creative. Not because you have to, but because you want to. Evolution is the secret for the next step. — *Karl Lagerfeld*

I also advise staying clear of a lot of prints. It is much easier to wear a great black or navy skirt more than once in a week without even the meanest of your colleagues noticing, but wear that printed dress twice in one week and you will look like you don't have anything else in your closet.

There is no magic formula as to how many pieces you need to have in your capsule wardrobe or what the pieces should be. If you are a trouser girl then why should you listen to someone who says you need to have at least two dresses in your collection? This is where your personal style shines through.

Everything you buy should be a piece that you love or at least that fulfils a purpose. I can't say I *love* my GAP three-quarter-sleeve T-shirt but I know it does the job when I put it on. I can say I love my favourite chunky knit cardigan because it makes me feel fabulous.

That is the difference between pieces and workhorse items. 'Pieces' are the clothes that make your style and lift your spirit. The workhorses are the basics such as black tights, great-fitting undergarments, jeans and T-shirts that hold their shape.

It is a good idea to stockpile your workhorse items. I always take advantage of sales when I stock up on tights, socks and T-shirts. I like to have a few in reserve, as you never know when one of your horses will need to be put out to pasture, aka the rag pile.

If you want to work with a capsule wardrobe, remember, the fewer items you have the more wear each one will get. I have been known to buy two pairs of the same boots because I liked them so much and I could not bear to be without them. You might feel the same about your perfectly fitting trousers: buy a spare pair – you won't regret it.

Building a wardrobe is an ongoing process; you really can't just go on one shopping expedition and expect to be finished. You are building your signature look that will make you feel confident in any situation.

The best pieces in your closet are like the best people in your life: you can rely on them, but you can also have a great time with them. — *Michael Kors*

I adore having a small wardrobe that works for me. Getting dressed in the morning is easy if you don't have too many choices. I tend to wear a lot of dresses. I love that I only have to put on one item then accessorize. Some people may prefer to wear a lot of separates. They may start with a suit then add a dress. If your lifestyle is more casual then perhaps start with a great pair of jeans, then add some tops and sweaters. Start with the item you are going to wear the most. This is a classic way to start building your capsule wardrobe.

Buy less, choose well & do it yourself! — *Vivienne Westwood*

You must take all the previous steps I talked about into consideration:

    1. What is your all-time favourite garment?

    2. Figure out your palette.

    3. Get a role model.

6. How to Shop

Don't be into trends. Don't make fashion own you, but you decide what you are, what you want to express by the way you dress and the way you live. — *Gianni Versace*

Say goodbye to cheap clothing

What is wrong with a little cheap-and-cheerful clothing? Every girl would like to get a new dress for Saturday night, right? Wrong! Don't we ever get tired of consuming? I know people who have so much stuff that they could not list a quarter of it.

We forsake the idea of owning a few, fabulous, quality pieces that could last for longer than two trips to the washing machine in favour of a closet full of one-time-only items. I personally have better things to do with my time than to trawl around the shops a couple of times a week.

I relish taking out my favourite cashmere sweater when the weather changes; it is like saying hello to an old friend. I can't really say the same for my winter coat which has given me almost ten years of loyal service. Yes, it is still stylish, Costume National, grey with a military feel, but I think that this year I might go wild and buy a new coat since I wore it day in and day out during last year's cold winter.

At the moment I am in the middle of a big decluttering project, which, as a former fashion stylist, is not easy. I have always been good at choosing the stylish over the trendy. I just can't seem to understand the desire to consume in cheap, fast fashion shops. I have a very good friend who buys super cheap ballet flats in what seems like bulk. Once a pair looks a bit scruffy (in about five wearings) she bins them and gets another pair. Is all this shopping for inexpensive clothing a false economy? Why would someone one want several pairs of cheap shoes when they could afford to buy one quality pair?

"It's better to have fewer things of quality than too much expendable junk. —Rachel Zoe

I am overjoyed when I find an item in my closet that is years old but still looks in great shape. This summer I rediscovered a black blazer, which I bought circa 1990 and it looked new to me again. Some things will stay in the closet longer than others and if you go for super-high-fashion items they either never really go out of style because they were never really in the style mainstream or they will look like a costume.

Fashion is cyclical and everything comes back again, so it is really worth in the long run buying clothes that are made of quality fabric with excellent workmanship when we can afford it. I know there are times we need a quick fix but we should not make it a regular thing.

Dress shabbily and they remember the dress; dress impeccably and they remember the woman. — **Coco Chanel**

What to spend the big money on

You should spend the most on your key items, the ones you wear the most – my list of what I am prepared to spend on is:

1. A good winter coat – That is, if you live in a place like the UK or the East Coast of America because you will be wearing it daily for several months. You can buy a great timeless one in one of the recurring trends such as military or vintage, or a just a well-made, fabulously fitting one: if you take care of it, it can last years

2. Boots – Another item you will be wearing a lot in the dark, cold winter months. Spend money on a simple, chic pair that will go with most of your wardrobe. If you

feel the need for a trendier pair in, say, leopard print, hit the high street as you probably won't want to keep them next year.

You can never take too much care over the choice of your shoes. Too many women think that they are unimportant, but the real proof of an elegant woman is what is on her feet. — *Christian Dior*

3. Handbag – Bags have turned into the barometer of being 'in the know': get one good one, which you can grab at a good consignment shop/dress agency for a fraction of the retail price. Your bag doesn't have to be from the current season: just make it a bag that you would want to carry for a while.

Luxury bags make your life more pleasant, make you dream, give you confidence, and show your neighbors you are doing well. — *Karl Lagerfeld*

7. Where to Shop

Forget the high street: make eBay your best friend

Do you like really nice things but not the retail price? Of course you do – who doesn't? One would have to be crazy to want to pay more for an item. Before I take out my debit card I always check eBay. You can buy almost anything on eBay, from an iPhone case to designer handbags to beauty products.

I know some people are afraid of getting ripped off when buying on eBay but if you do a little research into whom you are buying from and use a little common sense then the chance of it all going wrong goes down significantly.

What you can buy on eBay

Before I get into how to vet sellers, let's look at some of the fabulous items I have grabbed recently. My most recent purchase was a sold-out Marni bag. I got it for about 10% below retail and never had to leave my flat. I also buy quite a few of my cosmetics there as well. With cosmetics, as long as it is stated that they are new and in box (NIB in eBay speak, see Glossary) you will be OK. No one has tested it or even opened it.

Before placing a bid, I like to peruse my favourite beauty hall where I test all the colours, creams and smells; then I make my want list. Most big brands can be found on eBay and if you like more obscure brands you might have more luck on eBay than on the high street. For example, I scored some Private Label Tom Ford cologne (which is only sold at a few exclusive shops) for my beloved's birthday. I saved 13% off the retail price, including the shipping. Everybody wins: he smells good and I have a bit more in my pocket.

You are probably wondering where all these fabulous goods come from to be sold at a discount: some are unwanted gifts; some are left over stock from shops that are no longer trading; and some are from people who have shopped too much and are doing a clear-out. Some might even be from a magazine's beauty cupboard.

The other things I always buy on eBay is hair products; these I buy in industrial sizes, which means they are either coming from a salon or a distributor. I have bought some very expensive shampoo in such a big size that it brings the price down to that of a chemist's brand. The other great things about this are that you only have to buy shampoo twice a year and you have great-looking hair.

Finding your item/shipping cost/duty

When searching for your desired item, you can search

for items only in your own country or do a worldwide search. Of course, a worldwide search will bring many more choices but you must always factor in the shipping cost. If the shipping cost to your country is not clearly stated, it is always a good thing to email the seller for an exact figure. Many times any savings you might have made get swallowed up in the shipping cost.

The other thing you need to take into consideration when bidding on items from outside the EU is that you will be required to pay duty. Most sellers will not factor it in for you, so you may be hit with a large VAT bill and in the UK Customs always charge an £8 fee (at the time of writing) for the pleasure of processing your duty payment.

I try to steer clear of expensive items from the US for that reason, unless the item is something that I will never get on this side of the Atlantic. I do sometimes have things sent to my sister in the US to hold for me until I go over for a visit.

Now that you have the item you want to purchase in your sights, your next step is to investigate the seller. Always check out the seller's feedback; I don't deal with anyone who has less than ten feedback comments. You can get a pretty good idea of what the person is like to deal with by the comments. If the item is something you really want and no one else has it, use your judgement as to whether you want to take a risk. Everyone starts with a zero feedback rating so this seller could just be getting into the game or they could have messed up big time and have started all over again with a new account.

Paying for your item

Most sellers require you to have a PayPal account in order to pay them. PayPal is a web-based application for the secure transfer of funds between member accounts. PayPal uses your debit or credit card to pay for your item. PayPal is now owned by eBay, which is why most sellers require you to use it, as it makes the process much smoother and quicker than cheques or bank transfers.

Leaving feedback

eBay thinks of itself as a community so you are expected to be polite and to leave feedback when you finish a transaction. Never leave negative feedback unless you have gone through every channel of communication to settle the dispute. Negative feedback stays on your record until

you leave eBay, so never use negative feedback lightly.

Saved searches

The Saved Search tool is great when you are looking for a specific item. When you do an eBay search and the item you are looking for does not come up or you need a different size or colour, then there is a little app that enables you to save that specific search. This means that whenever the item you were searching for is listed in the future, you will receive an email. This is great if you are looking for anything rare or exotic.

eBay Glossary – eBay has a specific way of stating the condition of the listed item.

New with box aka NIB

A brand-new, unused, and unworn item (including handmade items) in the original packaging (such as the original box or bag) and/or with the original tags attached.

New without box aka NWOB

A brand-new, unused, and unworn item (including handmade items) that is not in original packaging or may be missing original packaging materials (such as the original box or bag). The original tags might not be attached. For example, new shoes (with absolutely no signs of wear) that are no longer in their original box fall into this category.

New with tags aka NWT

A brand-new, unused, and unworn item (including

handmade items) in the original packaging (such as the original box or bag) and/or with the original tags attached.

New without tags aka NWOT

A brand-new, unused, and unworn item (including handmade items) that is not in original packaging or may be missing original packaging materials (such as the original box or bag). The original tags might not be attached.

New with defects

A brand-new, unused, and unworn item. Possible cosmetic imperfections range from natural colour variations to scuffs, cuts or nicks, hanging threads or missing buttons, which occasionally occur during the manufacturing or delivery process. The apparel may contain irregular or mismarked size tags. The item may be missing the original packaging materials (such as original box or tag). New factory seconds and/or new irregular items may fall into this category. The original tags may or may not be attached. See the seller's listing for full details and description of any imperfections.

Pre-owned aka Used

An item that has been used or worn previously. See the seller's listing for full details and description of any imperfections.

Ebay has made it even easier to win your coveted items with their application for any mobile device. You can get notifications of auctions ending, make bids and even sell items when you are out and about.

I have been in a shop, found what I wanted to buy, located it on eBay, where it was less expensive and bought it on the spot with the 'Buy it Now' button. It could not be simpler.

8. How to Shop the Sales

Buy what you don't have yet, or what you really want, which can be mixed with what you already own. Buy only because something excites you, not just for the simple act of shopping. *— Karl Lagerfeld*

You must have nerves of steel to enter into sales shopping because it is a minefield of temptation and possible mistakes. I am not a very good sales shopper. I tend to get too excited by all the bargains, buy in haste and regret later. If you are going to shop the sales, there are a few rules.

1. Make a list – plan what you are looking to buy at the sales. Do not go hunting for random bargains: that is a recipe for overspending.

2. Do a recce (short for reconnaissance à la Jason Bourne) – before the sales begin: have a browse around and check prices. It is also good to locate where your desired items are in the store. If you are looking to add to your wardrobe make sure you try on anything that you like so you can note the correct size and eliminate the items that don't suit you.

I try to be extremely thorough on my recce. I make notes and take photos on my phone to remind me what I saw. I even take photos of clothing that I am trying on – sometimes an item will look less appealing to you a few hours later.

3. Edit your list – after you have completed your recce there will some things that you will want to add to your list and probably quite a few that you will want to eliminate. Make sure any clothing you buy will fit you: *never* buy something that you will have to slim down to fit in. Chances are, by the time you fit the item, you won't like it any more or you will resent having spent money on an item that you are not wearing.

4. Plan your sales attack – decide which shop you are going to start in. If you are looking for dresses or skirts wear tights, it will be easier to try dresses on. Also don't wear a lot of layers; you want to be able to try things on quickly.

Even if you have done the most thorough recce, give the sales floor another look, sometimes retailers will bring out special buys just for the sale that you might not have seen.

When buying clothes in the sales, always give them a good looking over: you don't want to buy your dream sweater to find it has an ink spot or a hole in it. People tend to manhandle merchandise much more in the sale environment.

When looking for a specific designer item such as an amazing handbag, be the first person at the door when the shop opens. Camping out is frowned upon as no handbag is worth frostbite.

5. Pack your kit bag – an army runs on its stomach: make sure you have a good breakfast, pack snacks and water as you do not want to be wasting precious time or money sitting in a cafe.

Wear comfortable shoes and leave the kids at home if you can.

6. Stick to the list – do not get caught up in the sales fury. The excitement can be contagious; you might want to get out the credit card when you see lots of other people spending like maniacs but remember, they will be waking up with the debt hangover. Stick to your list and stay within budget to have financially safe and fulfilling sales shopping.

9. What's Under the Hood

Lingerie or, what was called in the 1950s, foundation garments, are the key component to you looking your best.

Before you shop for anything, hit a reputable lingerie department. Wearing an ill-fitting or wrong-sized bra will destroy any of the admirable work in becoming a stylish gal.

I totally believe that lingerie should only come in two colours: black and nude. A white bra never looks good, even under a white shirt. It will pop, as in you will see the outline. This is even more important if you are a lady of colour.

To keep your silhouette looking good, get fitted for a new bra when you gain or lose weight, as fit is paramount to looking good in your clothes.

If you have maintained your size, it is still good to replace bras about every six months. They are made of elastic which is a natural fibre that perishes over time and will not continue to give the support required.

If you have a lot of money to spend or live a lifestyle that requires you to wear exciting lingerie then go right ahead. Buy fun colours, lots of lace, and prints, but if you wanting to look great in your clothes then buy the best you can afford in nude and black and take good care of it.

I also think decent hosiery is very important. I tend to buy matt opaque tights that don't shine too much: otherwise your legs might look like sausages. Stay away from tights with acrylic in them because they will bobble and fade quickly. It can be a false economy to buy the cheapest as you will probably be replacing them much sooner than if you bought ones of a bit better quality.

If you are looking for support or sucking in, I don't think you can beat Spanx. They are the Rolls-Royce of foundation garments at the moment. They are expensive but you can sometime find them a bit cheaper on eBay. They also last ages if you take care of them.

Hint: invest in a lingerie bag – this will help to keep your tights from snagging and your lingerie from getting pulled out of shape when they are in the in the washing machine.

10. Accessorize Like You Mean It

With the right accessories a woman can rule the world – I am sure that someone said that: if not, I just did.

Jewellery, scarves, shoes and handbags can completely change an outfit. If you look closely at Holly Golightly's wardrobe in *Breakfast at Tiffany's*, Audrey Hepburn wore only solid colours with statement jewellery.

A brightly coloured necklace can make your little black dress look completely different from when you are wearing it with some chandelier earrings and a bangle. The dress can change again if you wear it with boots and cardigan.

One is never over-dressed or underdressed with a Little Black Dress - *Karl Lagerfeld*

Accessories are a great investment. They don't 'not fit' if your weight changes, and if you get bored with them, they can be resold on eBay much more easily than an item of clothing.

Years ago, ladies did not have access to mass-manufactured, reasonably priced clothes, so they would use their talent of accessorizing to make their dresses look different. They used hats, scarves, jewellery, handbags and shoes to change their look.

I think dressing up or down should be a creative experience. Exciting. Fun. For me the key to personal style lies in accessories. I love objects from different worlds, different eras, combined my way. Never uptight, achieving – hopefully – a kind of throwaway chic — *Iris Apfel*

Accessories are a great way to expand a small or capsule wardrobe. I personally don't have a lot of clothes but I do have a weakness for handbags. I can feel totally different in a dress when I change my accessories and makeup. Never forget that makeup is a type of accessory.

Just think how different you feel when you put on your favourite red lipstick. You feel like you own the room.

11. What You Wear Every Day

Your face and hair

Besides spending on your boots, winter coat and a great handbag, you need to invest in your hair and your skin. Being well groomed is almost more important than being well dressed.

To reinvent a newly impeccable you in the most modern of outfits, don't skip on make-up and be sure to have flawless skin and hair. That will have more impact than expensive clothes. — *Karl Lagerfeld*

If you have a good hairdresser then you will never have a bad hair day and I cannot tell you what a joy that is. I believe in changing hairdressers until you find one that makes you feel great. Be brave: if you see someone with great hair, ask who they go to.

It is crucial to feel good about yourself whenever you leave your home; put on a bit of lipstick at least. You never know what is around the corner – a new job or the love of your life. Be ready for anything.

Hair and skin maintenance is essential because you wear your hair and face every day. A good haircut is crucial, as are regular trims.

If you don't feel you can afford to go to a good hairdresser, look for deals. Many salons do loyalty programmes, whereby if you book your next appointment on the day of your appointment, you get a discount. Some even do half-price colour on a Monday which is a real bargain.

Blond is a cruel mistress

Beware of buying into a hairstyle you can't really afford. It has happened to all of us: you are looking through the latest *Vogue* and you spot the hair that would make your life *perfect*.

What's the problem, you ask? It is a platinum-blond precision bob that would need to be touched up regularly every five weeks. That is an investment hairstyle. Do you have the funds and the time to go to the hairdresser every five weeks? Most probably not unless you are a celebrity, who's living depends on her hair.

OK, you are now ready to compromise on the blond bob. What you need to do is have a chat with your hairdresser, explaining your lifestyle and budget (both time and money). Stylists are getting much better with trying to find you a hairstyle that will fit your budgetary requirements and still look great.

If you need to colour your hair but don't have a huge beauty budget then go for a colour that is quite close to your natural one. The root regrowth won't require you to get it touched up as often. Stay away from high-maintenance super blond or super dark.

Beauty piggybank

I put a little bit of money aside every week into my beauty fund so I will always have the money when salon day comes around. It is good to put aside a bit of money for yourself, especially if you have a family and usually put your needs last.

My beauty fund encompasses hair maintenance, skin products and, if I have any money left, I treat myself to a facial.

Nature gives you the face you have at twenty. Life shapes the face you have at thirty. But at fifty you get the face you deserve. – *Coco Chanel*

The skin you are in

I think it is of the utmost importance to take good care of your skin. We get the face we deserve as we get older. Any lifestyle mistakes show, whether they be smoking, not getting enough rest or just not using eye cream; it will all show.

Taking regular care of your skin has been said to delay the signs of aging. *Always* take your makeup off before bed. Moisturize, moisturize, moisturize. Use eye cream. Get facials when you can afford them.

Don't think that you can neglect your skin and then do something radical, like have a facelift, later on. If you have not taken care of your skin, it might not be in good enough condition for the face lift to be viable. Scary thought, isn't it?

There are no ugly women, only lazy ones. — *Helena Rubinstein*

Makeup

A good red lipstick is an essential in every woman's cosmetic bag: it is a classic. Think about where you are going and who you will be meeting when planning your makeup. It is always better to stay on the conservative side, especially at work functions. If you are going to do a serious lip then go very light on the eye makeup.

Remember, trends in cosmetics change almost as much as in fashion so never make a forever commitment like permanent makeup, for example, eyebrow tattooing.

Beauty, to me, about being comfortable in your own skin. That, or a kick-ass red lipstick. — *Gwyneth Paltrow.*

12. Look Like You Are Rich, When You Aren't, Yet

Fake it till you can afford it

We have all heard the quote, 'dress for the job you want, not the one you have' and it is true – somewhat. When we dress for interviews or big events we need for people to understand our style language. We ideally like to look as though we belong there; we fit in.

Create your own style... let it be unique for yourself and yet identifiable for others.— *Anna Wintour*

There are a few items you should have on hand for such situations:

Diamond stud earrings – Always a classic and easy to fake until you can afford the real thing. Buy some good-quality Cubic Zirconia's, in a small size, say .20 of a carat: then, when you can afford the real thing, you can just replace them. No one will know the difference; just make sure the fakes are not so large that it would be unbelievable that they were real.

Watches – Don't wear a cheap watch: it is better to wear no watch at all. Watches have been an indicator of success since they were invented. Wait until you can get a good one. If you are one of those people who cannot live without a watch, then visit pawn shops to see if you can grab one on the cheap. One person's misfortune could be your lucky day.

Handbags – They have become the barometer of success during the past twenty years, since Prada came on the scene. If you can't afford a designer one, get the plainest nondescript bag you can. Don't buy a bag that is pretending to look like a designer bag; avoid labels and gold names plates because they will make you look as though you are trying too hard. Keep an eye out for your dream bag on eBay. Wealthy people tend to get rid of items that are in almost-new condition for a fraction of the retail price.

Shoes – Are very similar to handbags in that if you can't buy expensive, buy as simple as possible. Shoes are not as much of an indicator for women as they are for men because women are expected to have a bigger shoe collection. You can easily get away with only having a couple of pairs of good shoes until you have the funds to add to your collection.

Always buy the best you can or wait until you can afford your ideal items. As I said in the earlier chapter about a capsule wardrobe, if you keep your colour choices simple, you can get away with a minuscule wardrobe and add to it as and when you can.

Wear a good watch or none at all— *Jenna Lyons*

Adopt the habit of the well dressed

Well-dressed people take good care of their clothing and pretty much all their stuff. They buy expensive things and respect them.

Here are a few habits of a well-dressed person.

1. Do not wear your best items in the house. This means changing into more comfortable, perhaps casual, clothes when you get home from work.

Make this a ritual – get through the door and change into yoga gear, old jeans, whatever you are not worried about messing up while you are pottering around or cooking the dinner.

2. Everything has its place – shoes go back into their boxes with tissue, not kicked off and chucked under the bed.

3. When a handbag or pair of shoes comes with a dust-bag, use it. This means the manufacturer believes the item needs to be protected.

4. Rotate your best items – don't wear or use the same shoes or handbag every day. Change it up a bit and let your other things come out when appropriate.

5. Find a good cobbler or shoe repair person – this is vital to extending the life of your shoes and boots. Get the soles and heels replaced seasonally if you wear them often. A good shoe doctor can even dye your shoes if you want to change them for the next season.

If you can't locate a good shoe guy, ask in one of the better shoe stores like Prada, Louis Vuitton or Gucci. They usually do repairs for clients and have a seriously high standard of craftsmanship. You may end up paying a bit more than the guy down the street but it will be worth it.

6. Protect new coats with Scotchguard

7. Clean everything at the end of the season, especially winter coats, sweaters and anything made of natural fibres that moths would find tasty. Moths are more drawn to unwashed clothes, with perspiration or food on them.

Hand wash or dry-clean your precious items, then store them in vacuum-sealed bags for extra protection.

8. Plan what you are going to wear the night before: that's why well-dressed people look so calm in the morning.

9. When it comes to accessorizing, always take off one thing before you leave the house. There is no need for large earrings and a large necklace: wear one or the other. Figure out which piece you would like to be your focal point. That is, unless you are working the OTT (over the top) look.

I work to adopt these habits. A few have been ingrained in me since childhood – my Dad always changed out of his suit as soon as he got home and made sure everything was hung up neatly. I always change out of my street clothes when I get home.

13. Conclusion

I hope that after reading this you will want to develop your own personal style and give cheap clothing a miss. It is a joy to buy quality if you are clever, which I know you are since you bought this book.

I have peppered this book with quotes from famous fashionable people so I thought I would put a few of my own in.

A few words of my wisdom

Always try to look your best when you leave the house, no matter if you are just running to the corner for milk – you never know who you might meet.

Dress for who you want to be.

Buy the best you can afford.

Treat your clothes and accessories like good friends: take care of them and they will take care of you.

Dress for the job you want, not the one you have.

Always give yourself a once-over in a full-length mirror before you leave the house.

Why be a clone of a celebrity when you can be the original stylish you? I will leave you with my most favourite quote of all time –

"Life's a banquet and most poor suckers are starving to death!" — Auntie Mame

About the Author

I have worked in the fashion industry for over 20 years. I have worked in London and New York as a stylist, personal shopper and Fashion Week show producer.

In my style journey, I know that some seasons the shapes and colours might not suit me, so I just ignore what the so-called fashion gurus are saying, and go back to knowing what works for me.

I have written for various websites including the feature 'How to get everything cheaper' that appeared in the July 2012 issue of Glamour UK.
I am an ex-Manhattanite who now lives very happily in London.

Thank You

Thanks for buying and taking the time to read *Style NOT Fashion.*

If you have enjoyed and found this book useful, I would be honoured if you could give me a review on the Amazon book page.

Printed in Great Britain
by Amazon.co.uk, Ltd.,
Marston Gate.